Echoes of Economic Eruptions
A Comprehensive Guide

Tracing the History of
Financial Crashes and Bubbles
from
Tulip Mania to the Digital Age

Artenie Alexandru

ISBN: 9798867334444

Table of Contents

Disclaimer

The information provided in this book is for general educational and informational purposes only and should not be construed as financial advice.

Any investment or financial decisions you make based on information provided in this book are made solely at your own risk.

We do not provide personalized investment advice or recommend or endorse specific investments, products, services, or strategies.

You should consult a financial advisor or professional before making investment decisions.

All investments come with risks and may lose value.

Past performance is not indicative of future results.

Any views expressed in this book are those of the individual author.

The provided content is not intended to be a solicitation or offer to buy or sell securities or financial instruments.

Foreword

"Why write a book about crashes?" you might say. Well, history can be a good teacher. By analyzing past events, you can acquire some wisdom that will prevent you from making catastrophic mistakes and losing your money.

> *"The four most dangerous words in investing are, it's different this time."* — Sir John Templeton (investor, banker, fund manager, and philanthropist).

That is absolutely true. As you will see throughout the book and in the conclusion, there are some patterns that repeat themselves in most cases.

I invite you on this journey and encourage you to learn the lessons of the past to achieve a brighter future.

Fasten your seat belt, and let's go!

Artenie Alexandru, Iasi, 2023

www.art-invest.net

1. Introduction

Navigating the Storms of Financial Crises

Throughout history, money and the way we handle it have shaped the world. It's like a powerful force that can bring great prosperity or great disaster. This book is about those moments when things go wrong, when the world of money falls apart. We're going to explore these events called "financial crashes."

A financial crash happens when the world of money gets all messed up. It's like a giant tangle of threads, and suddenly it unravels. People lose their savings, businesses go under, and it feels like everything is falling apart.

We're starting our journey into this world of financial crashes by going way back in time. First, we'll look at the "Tulip Mania" of 1637. This was when people went crazy for tulip flowers, and their prices shot up. But then, just as quickly, they crashed, and people lost a lot of money. It's a story about how people can get carried away and make bad decisions when it comes to money.

Next, we'll travel to the early 1700s and the "South Sea Bubble." This was a time when people in England got excited about investing in a company's stock, and it became a big deal. But, like a bubble, it burst, leaving a lot of people in trouble. This event is a lesson about the dangers of getting caught up in investments that sound too good to be true.

As we move forward in time, we'll meet the "Panic of 1837" in the United States. This was a time when banks failed, and the economy was in chaos. It showed us that when a country is growing and changing, it can be vulnerable to financial problems. It was also a time when people were coming up with new ways to deal with money, but it didn't always work out.

The next chapters will take us through some big financial disasters like the "Great Depression" of 1929, the "dot-com bubble" of the early 2000s, and the "global financial crisis" of 2008. These events were like earthquakes in the world of money, and they had a huge impact on people's lives. They made us realize how risky investments, new financial ideas, and too much borrowing can lead to disaster.

In these stories, we'll also learn about the complicated world of modern finance. We'll see how all these different financial markets, complex financial products, and taking on too much debt can make things go really wrong.

But financial crashes aren't just about numbers and markets. They're also about people and how they act. We'll look at why people sometimes act like a herd, all doing the same thing, even if it's a bad idea. We'll see how people can become overconfident and make risky choices. And we'll learn how fear can spread like wildfire and cause a lot of damage.

This journey is not just about the past; it's also about today and what might happen in the future. The world of money is changing, with things like digital currencies and new technology. We'll explore these new challenges and how they might affect our financial future.

This book is not just a history lesson. It's a chance to understand why financial crashes happen and how we might stop them. We'll talk about rules and laws that try to keep the financial world safe. But we'll also talk about personal responsibility – how we all play a part in keeping our money safe.

So, come with me on this journey. We'll travel through the ups and downs of financial history and think about some big questions. Why do financial crashes happen, and can we stop them? What role do rules and laws play, and when do we need to take responsibility for our own financial choices? Financial crashes may be a part of our world, but they also teach us a lot about ourselves and how we handle money.

2. A Historical Odyssey Through Financial Crises

To understand the essence of financial crashes, we must embark on a historical odyssey, tracing the evolution of these economic cataclysms through the annals of time. From the bustling marketplaces of ancient civilizations to the intricacies of the modern global financial system, our journey reveals the enduring cycle of financial booms and busts, each imbued with unique characteristics but sharing common threads of human behavior and economic consequences.

2.1. Early Antecedents: Rome, Greece, and Beyond

In the heart of ancient Rome, a sprawling and bustling metropolis, the financial markets of the day were alive with activity. Trading in goods, real estate, and commodities was not without its risks. The value of assets could fluctuate dramatically, often influenced by the vagaries of supply and demand. In such a dynamic economic environment, financial disasters were not uncommon. Speculative excess and unbridled risk-taking could result in personal ruin and, at times, social trouble.

Figure 1 - Denarius featuring emperor Marcus Aurelius[1]

Ancient Greece, another cradle of civilization, had its share of financial crises. The maritime city-states of Greece engaged in extensive trade, and the intricacies of this commerce sometimes led to market instability. Agricultural goods, often subject to unpredictable weather conditions, would fluctuate in value, affecting the livelihoods of many.

Figure 2 - Ancient Greek Coinage[2]

These early episodes of economic turmoil provide insights into the vulnerabilities of financial systems based on trust and the inherent risks of economic interconnectedness.

The financial crises of ancient times might differ in detail from those of the modern era, but they share common threads. In Rome and Greece, as in later periods, **speculation** was an ever-present force. The allure of **quick riches** and the desire for status could lead to irrational exuberance and, in turn, to precipitous declines in wealth and economic stability. These early antecedents serve as stark reminders that the age-old motivations for financial excess and recklessness have been constant companions to the story of finance.

Though separated by millennia, these ancient financial crises resonate with the narratives of modern times. The temptation of speculation, the pitfalls of overleveraging, and the fragility of financial systems underpin the enduring cycles of boom and bust that we continue to witness in the ever-evolving world of finance.

As we move forward in our historical journey through financial crises, we'll encounter the birth of modern finance in the Dutch Republic and the emergence of financial markets, exploring how these developments set the stage for the crashes, bubbles, and busts of centuries to come.

2.2. The Tulip Mania: A Blooming Madness

Our journey into the history of financial crashes brings us to the early 17th century, to the bustling and vibrant Dutch Republic, where we encounter one of the most famous and extraordinary speculative episodes in the history of finance: *the Tulip Mania*. This peculiar event, often referred to as "Tulpenmanie" in Dutch, represents a captivating chapter in the story of human folly, greed, and the intoxicating allure of market speculation.

Figure 3 - Dutch Tulip Bulb Market Bubble[3]

The Dutch Golden Age and the Emergence of Tulipomania

The backdrop for the Tulip Mania was the Dutch Golden Age, a period of remarkable economic growth and cultural flourishing in the 17th century. The Dutch Republic had become a global economic powerhouse, driven by its naval dominance and international trade networks. This newfound prosperity gave rise to an affluent merchant class, who sought not only financial success but also the pleasures of life.

In this context, the cultivation of tulips became a popular pastime among the Dutch elite. The tulip, a foreign import from the Ottoman Empire, captured the imagination of the Dutch, who marveled at the flower's vibrant colors and intricate patterns. The tulip's allure extended beyond its aesthetic appeal; it was also seen as a status symbol, and owning rare and exotic tulip bulbs became a mark of prestige.

The Tulip Futures Market: A Novel Financial Innovation

The first sign of the Tulip Mania's approach was the creation of a novel financial instrument known as the tulip futures contract. This innovation allowed buyers to secure the delivery of tulip bulbs at a later date, with the prices for future deliveries determined in the present. It's worth noting that the tulip futures market was an unregulated, informal market, bearing little resemblance to the sophisticated financial instruments of today. Yet, it would play a pivotal role in the ensuing frenzy.

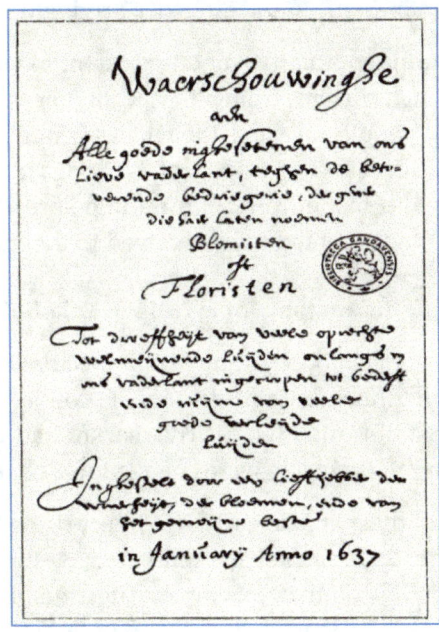

Figure 4 - Futures Contracts During Tulip Mania[4]

These futures contracts began as a pragmatic means for tulip growers to hedge against price fluctuations, ensuring that they would receive a fair price for their bulbs at the end of the growing season. However, the appeal of these contracts quickly spread beyond the flower beds. Speculators, drawn by the promise of substantial profits, began trading these tulip futures in earnest.

The Birth of Speculative Excess

The early phases of the Tulip Mania were marked by genuine interest in the tulip trade, with a focus on the bulbs themselves. Buyers purchased tulip futures contracts with the intention of taking physical delivery of the bulbs upon maturity. However, as the mania intensified, many participants in the market were no longer interested in tulips for their gardens but solely for financial gain.

The prices of tulip bulbs began to rise sharply, fueled by a speculative frenzy. Rare and exotic tulips could command staggering sums. In 1634, for example, one record reports that a single Viceroy tulip bulb was sold for a price equivalent to what a skilled craftsman might earn in an entire year. Buyers, often motivated by the fear of missing out on potential profits, eagerly entered the market, further driving up prices.

The impact of this speculative madness extended beyond the world of finance. Many Dutch citizens, from all walks of life, were caught up in the frenzy. Ordinary people invested their life savings in tulip bulbs, and many began trading in the hopes of striking it rich. The tales of extraordinary wealth made from tulip trading spread like wildfire, and soon, almost everyone seemed to be involved in the tulip market.

The Anatomy of a Tulip Mania Bubble

Tulip Mania was a textbook example of a speculative bubble. As prices climbed ever higher, they bore no reasonable connection to the intrinsic value of the tulip bulbs themselves. The market had detached from any fundamentals, and participants were engaged in a collective delusion.

At the height of the mania in early 1637, the price of a single tulip bulb, the Semper Augustus, reached a zenith that is almost beyond belief. Historical records tell us that a Semper Augustus bulb was sold for a staggering sum—equivalent to the price of a luxurious mansion in Amsterdam. Yet, as the bubble expanded, there was no shortage of willing buyers, each hoping to sell at an even higher price.

Figure 5 - Semper Augustus Tulip.[5]

The bubble eventually burst, and the consequences were profound. The tipping point was marked by an unsuccessful tulip bulb auction in Haarlem in February 1637. This event sparked a crisis of confidence among tulip traders, and suddenly, selling became the dominant sentiment. Prices began to plummet, leaving speculators who had invested their fortunes in tulips facing financial ruin.

The Aftermath: A Lesson in Financial Exuberance

In the aftermath of the Tulip Mania, Dutch society was left grappling with the consequences of this extraordinary speculative fever. Many were financially ruined, their fortunes wiped out by the collapse of tulip prices. The Dutch government, recognizing the need to restore order to the financial system, took measures to unwind the tulip futures contracts and to limit the damage.

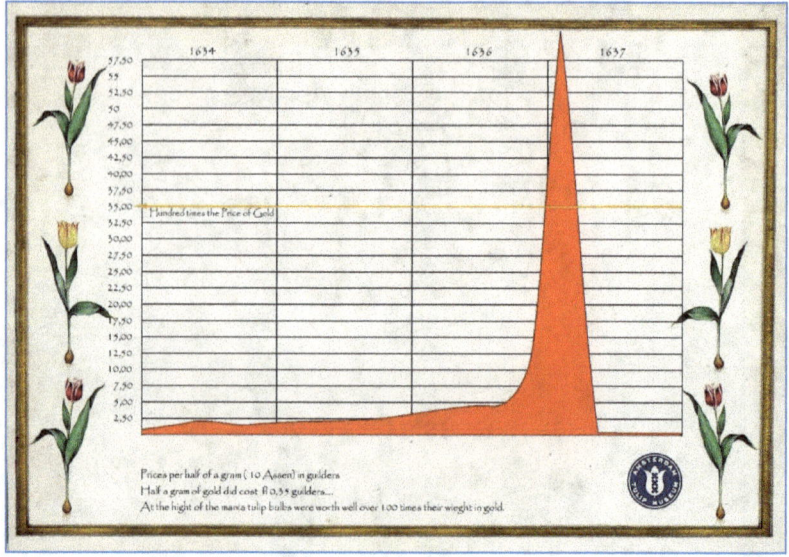

Figure 6 - Price Of Tulips During Tulip Mania[6]

In time, the memory of Tulip Mania became a cautionary tale, serving as a warning about the dangers of **speculative excess** and the irrationality of market behavior. The Dutch financial system, like many others in the wake of a financial crisis, evolved to introduce greater regulatory controls and protections.

Yet, despite the financial and social upheaval that the Tulip Mania caused, it remains a fascinating episode in financial history. It offers a window into the enduring aspects of human nature—our proclivity for speculation, our susceptibility to herd behavior, and our insatiable desire for wealth. The story of the Tulip Mania reminds us that the lessons of history are not always learned and that even in the most extraordinary of circumstances, the same patterns of exuberance and excess can reappear, a testament to the enduring nature of the human spirit in the world of finance.

2.3. The South Sea Bubble: A Tale of Wild Speculation

In the early 18th century, something extraordinary and disastrous happened in London's financial world. This event is known as the South Sea Bubble. It's a fascinating story of people getting carried away with dreams of making a lot of money, and it serves as a warning about the dangers of getting too caught up in the excitement of the stock market.

How It All Began

The South Sea Company started in 1711 with a mission to help the British government deal with its massive debt. They came up with a plan: they would take over a big chunk of the government's debt in exchange for the exclusive rights to trade in the South Seas, which included the profitable slave trade.

Figure 7 - Arms of the South Sea Company[7]

People were excited about this idea. They thought they could make good money by investing in the South Sea Company. They believed that this was a safe and profitable investment because the government would guarantee it. However, what happened next was beyond anyone's wildest imagination.

The Bubble Starts to Inflate

In 1719, the South Sea Company offered a new deal. They said that if you gave them government debt, they would give you shares of their company. People thought this was a surefire way to get rich. They saw the opportunity for unimaginable profits. The idea of being able to turn government debt into valuable shares in the company was too tempting to resist.

This sparked a buying frenzy. People were eager to buy shares in the South Sea Company. But this excitement didn't stop at just one company. Other businesses jumped on the bandwagon, and their shares were also in high demand. The stock market in London became a place of chaos, with people rushing to buy shares in whatever company promised the biggest profits.

A Market Gone Wild

The South Sea Bubble was a classic example of a speculative bubble. This is when the price of something goes way beyond what it's really worth. The stock prices were no longer connected to how well the companies were doing but were driven by people's belief that prices would keep going up forever.

At its peak in 1720, a share of the South Sea Company was worth an incredible £1,000. This was a huge jump from the £128 it was worth just a few months earlier. People were buying shares not because they thought the company was doing well but because they believed the price would keep rising. It was like a big party where everyone thought they were going to get rich.

Cheating and Lies

What makes the South Sea Bubble even more interesting is that a lot of people were cheating and lying to make it grow. The leaders of the South Sea Company and others spread false information about how much money they were making from their activities in the South Seas. They made things sound much better than they really were. This was all a trick to make people invest even more money.

Not only were private people involved, but some government officials were also part of this big lie. Some of these politicians had invested a lot of money in the South Sea Company, and they used their power to make sure the bubble kept growing.

Sir Isaac Newton did invest a significant amount of money in the South

Sea Company, but he sold his shares at a profit before the bubble burst. Later, he re-entered the market at a much higher price and suffered heavy losses, losing around £20,000 (equivalent to several million dollars today). This incident led him to famously remark, "I can calculate the motion of heavenly bodies, but not the madness of people."

The Bubble Bursts

It was clear to some people that this couldn't go on forever. The prices were just too high. In the summer of 1720, reality started to set in, and people began to sell their shares. This led to a panic, and the market started to crash.

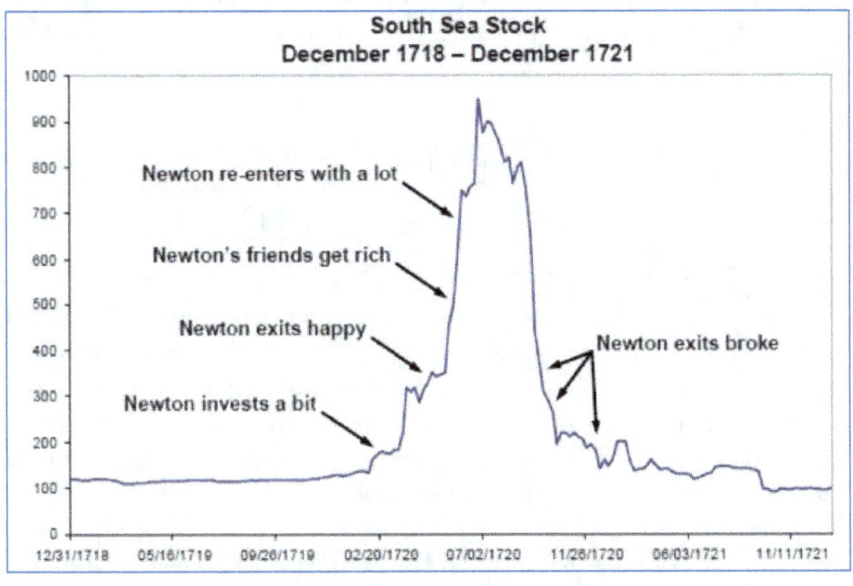

Figure 8 - Newton's South Sea Bubble Investment[8]

The bursting of the South Sea Bubble was a disaster. Many people lost a lot of money. They had invested their life savings, and it was all gone. People were furious, and they wanted someone to fix the situation.

The government stepped in and passed a law called the Bubble Act in 1720. This law made it much harder to create new companies and sell their shares without government approval. It was a way to prevent another speculative bubble like the South Sea Bubble from happening.

The Lessons of the South Sea Bubble

The South Sea Bubble is a reminder of how people can get carried away with dreams of getting rich quickly. It also shows us how important it is to have rules in place to make sure that the stock market is fair and safe. The South Sea Bubble left a lasting mark on the world of finance, and it teaches us to be cautious, to think carefully before investing our money, and to keep a close eye on those who promise easy riches.

In the chapters ahead, we'll explore more stories of financial crashes, each with its own lessons about the ups and downs of the financial world. From the excitement of speculative bubbles to the hard lessons learned after financial disasters, these historical events offer wisdom and warnings for those who navigate the sometimes turbulent waters of finance.

2.4.   The Panic of 1837: When Money Troubles Hit Home

Travel with us back to the early 19th century, to a time when the United States was a young and rapidly changing country. It was a time of big dreams and big challenges. In the midst of all this change, the nation faced an economic crisis known as the Panic of 1837. This event had a profound impact on the lives of ordinary people and provided a valuable lesson in the complexities of economic ups and downs.

America in the 1830s: A Land of Promise and Transformation

In the 1830s, the United States was a nation full of promise and potential. The country was growing fast, with people moving westward, opening up new lands, and building new cities. The invention of the steam locomotive and other technologies was changing the way people lived and worked.

With all this growth and change, banks and businesses were popping up all over the place. People were excited about the possibilities, and they wanted to be part of this new world of opportunity.

The Role of Banks and Paper Money

Banks played a significant role in this new world. They were places where people could save their money, borrow money to start businesses, and trade in a new form of currency called "paper money." This paper money wasn't like the paper bills we have today; it was often issued by local banks and was more like a promise to pay real gold and silver.

Figure 9 - 2 Dollars - Salem & Philadelphia Manufacturing, USA (1820's-1830's)

These banks and the paper money they issued made it easier for people to buy and sell things, invest in businesses, and fuel the growing economy. But there was a catch. The value of this paper money depended on people's trust in the banks and their ability to back up their promises with real gold and silver.

The Recipe for Panic: Speculation and Lending Frenzy

With banks issuing paper money, a sense of opportunity was in the air. People started buying and selling land, investing in new businesses, and speculating on all sorts of things. Speculation means taking risks in the hope of making a big profit. People were buying land, goods, and even more paper money in the hopes that they would become more valuable.

Banks also got into the mix. They were lending money to people for all sorts of ventures, sometimes without enough security or real assets to back up the loans. This lending frenzy created a situation where people were borrowing and spending more than they could afford, much like maxing out a credit card.

The Trigger: Economic Changes and International Troubles

Then, in the late 1830s, the economic picture changed. The United States faced challenges at home and abroad. The country experienced a series of economic shocks, including a downturn in the agricultural sector. Many farmers were facing hard times, and this ripple effect was felt throughout the economy.

Internationally, things got complicated, too. The United Kingdom, a major trading partner, was facing its own financial problems. This international uncertainty spilled over into the United States, causing people to lose confidence in the value of American paper money.

The Panic Begins: A Rush for Gold and Silver

This loss of confidence set off a panic. People began to lose trust in the paper money issued by banks. They started rushing to the banks to exchange their paper money for real gold and silver. It was like a game of musical chairs, with everyone scrambling to get a seat before the music stopped.

Figure 10 – Gold on Paper Money[9]

This rush for gold and silver drained the banks of their reserves, and many banks were not able to meet the demands of their customers. As a result, several banks closed their doors, leaving people who had their money in those banks in a very tough spot.

The Fallout: Hardships for Many

The Panic of 1837 had far-reaching consequences. Many people lost their savings and their jobs. Businesses shut down, and the economy went into a deep recession. People's dreams of prosperity turned into nightmares of poverty.

Even the government was affected. The U.S. government had been putting money into a national bank, hoping to keep the economy stable. But that bank had to close because of the panic, and the government's finances were thrown into chaos.

The panic led to a long and slow recovery. People had to pick up the pieces and start over. New banks emerged, and new financial systems were put in place to prevent such a crisis from happening again.

Lessons Learned: The Importance of Stability

The Panic of 1837 teaches us a valuable lesson about the importance of stability in the financial system. When banks and individuals take too many risks and when trust in the value of money disappears, it can lead to a financial crisis that affects everyone.

It also reminds us of the ups and downs of economic cycles. Even in times of progress and growth, there can be sudden changes that disrupt our lives. The Panic of 1837 is a story of how excitement and optimism can quickly turn to fear and hardship when the financial system is not well-managed.

In the chapters ahead, we will continue to explore more stories of financial crashes, each offering its own lessons about the world of finance.

2.5. The Great Depression: When Times Got Really Tough

Picture yourself in the late 1920s, a time of fancy cars, jazz music, and dreams of a bright future. But then, suddenly, everything changed. The Great Depression hit, and it was a period of tremendous hardship and struggle for people all over the United States. Let's go back in time and explore this difficult chapter in history.

The Roaring Twenties: A Time of High Hopes

The 1920s were known as the Roaring Twenties. It was a time when people felt optimistic and full of hope. New inventions like cars and radios made life exciting, and people enjoyed the thrill of the stock market.

Figure 11 - Duesenberg Model J (1928)

The stock market was like a big game where people bought and sold pieces of companies, hoping to make money. People believed that the stock market could only go up, and many invested their savings in it. They thought they were going to get rich quickly.

The Crash: A Sudden Fall

But in October 1929, something terrible happened. The stock market crashed. This meant that the prices of stocks fell very quickly, and people lost a lot of money. It was like a big balloon bursting.

The stock market crash had a big impact on people's lives. Many who had invested their savings in the stock market lost everything. People who thought they were wealthy suddenly found themselves with almost nothing.

As the Great Depression unfolded, things got worse. Many businesses couldn't make money, so they had to lay off workers. People who had jobs one day were suddenly out of work. The country faced massive unemployment, which meant many people were without jobs and income to support their families.

Life became really tough. Families struggled to put food on the table, and they couldn't afford to pay their bills. Some people even lost their homes because they couldn't pay their mortgages. It was a time of hardship, and people had to make do with very little.

Figure 12 - Monthly S&P 500 Returns, 1920-1939[10]

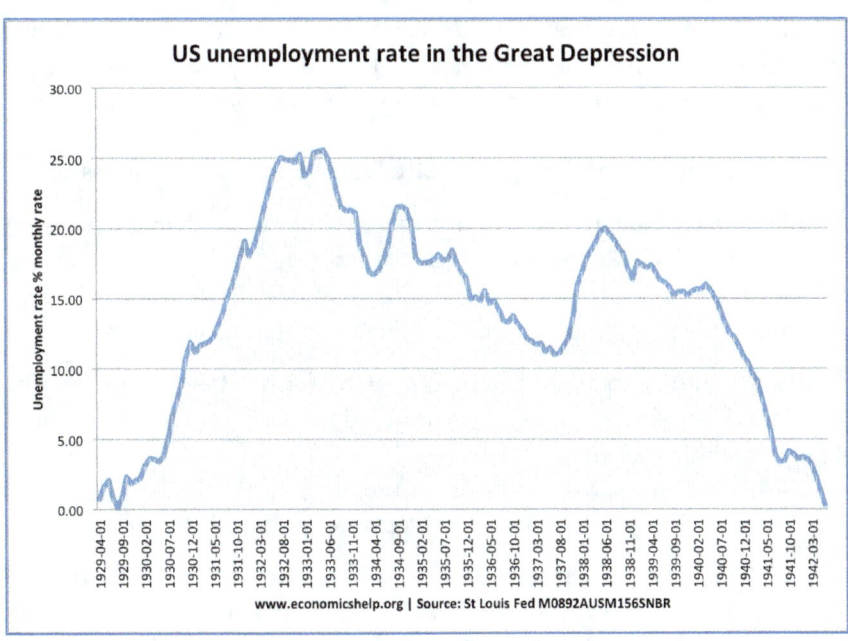

Figure 13 - Unemployment during the great depression[11]

Dust Bowl: Nature's Fury

Adding to the troubles of the Great Depression, there was an environmental disaster called the Dust Bowl. This was a period of severe drought and dust storms in the central United States, particularly in Oklahoma, Texas, Kansas, and surrounding areas. Crops failed, and the land turned to dust. Many families who relied on farming for their livelihoods suffered greatly.

Government Help: FDR's New Deal

In the midst of all this hardship, the U.S. government stepped in to help. President Franklin D. Roosevelt, often called FDR, introduced a series of programs known as the New Deal. These programs aimed to provide relief, recovery, and reform.

The relief part of the New Deal was about helping people right away. The government provided jobs through programs like the Civilian Conservation Corps and offered financial assistance to those in need.

The recovery aspect focused on getting the economy back on track. This included efforts to rebuild infrastructure and boost the country's financial health.

The reform part of the New Deal aimed to prevent another economic disaster like the Great Depression. New laws and regulations were put in place to make sure the financial system was more stable and fair.

Rebuilding and Resilience: Life During the Great Depression

Life during the Great Depression was hard, but people showed incredible resilience. Families stuck together and helped one another. Many people found creative ways to make ends meet, whether it was through growing their own food, bartering, or taking on odd jobs.

People also turned to entertainment to escape their troubles. The movies were a popular way to forget the harsh reality of life, and Hollywood thrived during this time.

The End of the Great Depression: World War II

The Great Depression finally came to an end in the late 1930s, but not because of the New Deal alone. It was the outbreak of World War II that helped pull the United States out of its economic troubles. The war effort created jobs and increased demand for goods and services, helping to revive the economy.

Lessons Learned: The Importance of Caution and Planning

The Great Depression teaches us important lessons. It shows us that the good times don't last forever. Just as in life, there are ups and downs in the economy. It also emphasizes the importance of having a safety net in place to help people when things get tough.

The stock market crash and the Great Depression have shaped how we think about the economy and finance. They've led to important changes in the way we manage money and plan for hard times.

2.6. The 1973 Oil Crisis: Fueling a World of Change

Imagine a time when you drove to the gas station, filled up your car's tank, and it didn't cost you a fortune. Gasoline was cheap and plentiful, and people didn't worry much about energy. That was the world before the 1973 oil crisis. But in 1973, everything changed, and we're going to take a journey back in time to understand how and why it happened.

The Beginning: The Yom Kippur War

In October 1973, something called the Yom Kippur War broke out in the Middle East. It was a conflict between Israel and a group of Arab countries, and it caused a lot of tension. The war started during a time when many Jewish people celebrated a holiday called Yom Kippur, and that's why it's called the Yom Kippur War.

During the war, the Arab countries involved were upset with the United States and other Western countries. They thought these countries were helping Israel, and they didn't like that. So, in response, they decided to use something as a weapon: oil.

The Oil Weapon: An Embargo

Now, what's this thing called an "embargo"? It's like when someone refuses to sell you something. In this case, several Arab countries, who were part of a group called OPEC (Organization of the Petroleum

Exporting Countries), said, "We're not going to sell oil to the United States and a few other countries that support Israel in this war." They called this an oil embargo.

This was a big deal because many countries, including the United States, depended on oil from the Middle East. It powered cars, factories, and just about everything that needed energy. So when the oil suddenly stopped flowing, it caused a lot of problems.

Gas Lines and Shortages: A New Reality

With the oil embargo in place, the United States faced a major challenge. Oil imports were cut, and this led to shortages of gasoline and other oil-related products. People had to wait in long lines at gas stations, and some stations even ran out of fuel. Can you imagine having to wait in line for hours just to get gas for your car?

Figure 14 - Connecticut filling station during the energy crisis[12]

The shortages and long lines were a big inconvenience, but it was just the beginning of the oil crisis's impact. Gas prices started to rise, and they went up fast. People had to pay a lot more for gas, which meant they had less money for other things.

Energy Conservation: Turning Down the Heat and Driving Less

As the oil crisis deepened, people were encouraged to save energy.

That meant turning down the heat in their homes and using less electricity. It also meant driving less and carpooling, which is when people share rides in one car instead of everyone driving separately. Some folks even started riding bicycles to work.

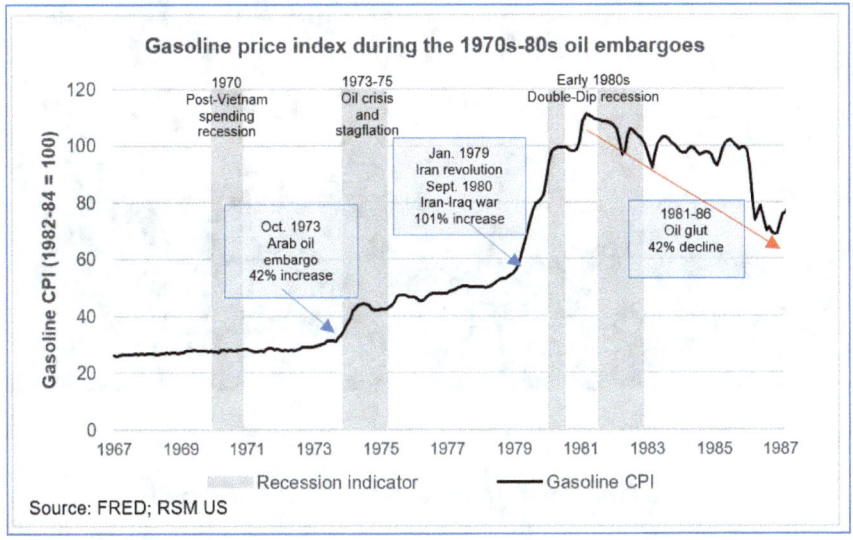

Figure 15 – Gasoline Price Index during the 1970s-80s[13]

You might wonder why energy conservation was so important. Well, the United States relied heavily on foreign oil, and when that oil became scarce, it became clear how much the country depended on it. Energy conservation was a way to make the limited oil supplies last longer and reduce the impact of the crisis.

New Car Designs: Smaller and More Efficient

Car companies started making changes to their vehicles in response to the oil crisis. Before the crisis, many cars were large and not very fuel-efficient. But as gas prices went up and people wanted to save on fuel costs, carmakers began producing smaller, more fuel-efficient cars.

One famous car from this time was the Volkswagen Beetle. It was a small, compact car that used less gas. People liked it because it was cheaper to drive, and it became an icon of the era.

Figure 16 - 1973 1303/Super Beetle[14]

The Strategic Petroleum Reserve: A Backup Plan

To prevent a future energy crisis like the one in 1973, the U.S. government started something called the Strategic Petroleum Reserve. It's like a big savings account for oil. The government stored large amounts of oil underground in various locations to use in case of emergencies, like another oil crisis or a natural disaster.

Figure 17 - United States Strategic Petroleum Reserves[15]

A New Focus on Renewable Energy: Solar Panels and Wind Turbines

The oil crisis made people think about where their energy came from and how to use it more wisely. It sparked an interest in renewable energy sources, like the sun and the wind. People began installing solar panels on their homes to harness the power of the sun, and wind turbines started to appear in some areas to generate electricity. These were early steps toward a more sustainable and diverse energy future.

The oil crisis didn't last forever. Negotiations between the warring parties in the Middle East led to a ceasefire, and the oil embargo was lifted. Things started to get back to normal, but the experience left a lasting impact.

The crisis led to changes in U.S. energy policy. The country began to focus more on energy independence and security, including efforts to reduce reliance on foreign oil. It also encouraged research and development in energy-efficient technologies and renewable energy sources.

Lessons Learned: The Importance of Diverse Energy Sources

The 1973 oil crisis taught us some important lessons. It showed us that depending too much on one source of energy, like foreign oil, can make us vulnerable to unexpected disruptions. It emphasized the importance of having a diverse mix of energy sources to reduce risk and increase resilience. The crisis also highlighted the need for energy conservation and the development of more efficient technologies.

In the chapters that follow, we'll continue to explore more stories of financial crises and economic challenges, each offering its own lessons about the world of finance and economics.

2.7. The Dot-Com Bubble: The Internet's Wild Ride

Welcome to the late 1990s, a time when the internet was the hottest thing around. People were flocking to the World Wide Web, and investors were eager to jump on the Internet bandwagon. This excitement gave rise to a financial phenomenon known as the Dot-Com Bubble, a thrilling yet turbulent chapter in financial history that we're about to explore.

The Internet Revolution: The Birth of the Dot-Coms

Back in the late 1990s, the internet was like a wild, uncharted frontier. It was a place where people could connect, share information, and shop online. It was the era of dial-up internet connections and websites with flashy, eye-catching designs.

During this time, numerous companies were founded to take advantage of the Internet's potential. These companies were often referred to as "dot-coms" because their website addresses typically ended with ".com." They had exciting and sometimes quirky names, and they offered all kinds of online services, from e-commerce to news to social networking. It was an era of bold ideas and even bolder investments.

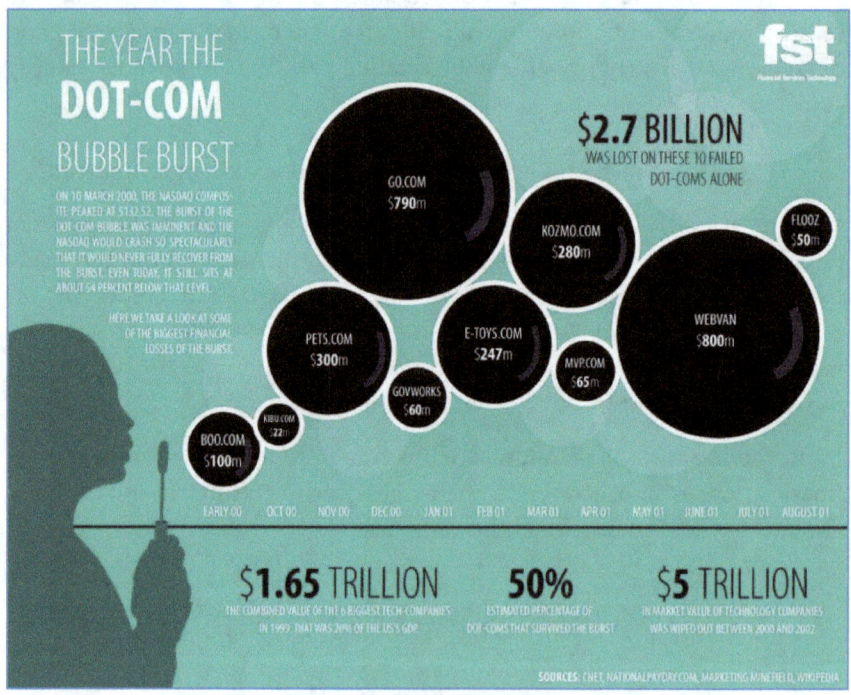

Figure 18 – The year the DOT-COM bubble burst[16]

The Hype: Soaring Stock Prices

The Dot-Com Bubble was fueled by a frenzy of excitement and optimism. Investors believed that these internet companies were the future, and they were willing to pour money into them. As a result, the stock prices of many dot-com companies skyrocketed to incredible heights.

People were buying shares of these companies, believing they would become millionaires overnight. It was a bit like a gold rush. Everyone wanted a piece of the internet action, and the market couldn't get enough of these stocks.

Investors weren't just buying shares; they were also trading them at a furious pace. Speculation was running wild. People were snapping up stocks not because they believed in the companies or their profits but because they thought they could sell them to someone else at a higher price.

Eye-Popping IPOs: Initial Public Offerings

One of the most exciting parts of the Dot-Com Bubble was the Initial Public Offering (IPO) frenzy. This is when a company goes from being privately owned to selling its shares to the public for the first time. Dot-com companies were having IPOs left and right, and these events were like grand parties on Wall Street.

Companies like Amazon and eBay had some of the most famous IPOs during this time. Their share prices surged on the first day of trading, and many investors made a lot of money. But it was also a sign of the speculative madness that was taking hold of the stock market.

Many of these dot-com companies had big dreams but little in the way of actual profits. They were focused on growth and market share, not on making money. Investors believed that these companies could worry about profits later; for now, it was all about capturing the new frontier of the internet.

The Bursting Bubble: Reality Sets In

But as the saying goes, "What goes up must come down." And that's exactly what happened. In the early 2000s, reality began to set in. Investors started to question whether the stock prices of these dot-com companies were justified.

Many of these companies were burning through cash without any clear path to profitability. The market started to realize that not all these dot-coms were going to become the giants they had hoped for. It was like the party was over, and now it was time to clean up.

As the enthusiasm waned, dot-com stock prices took a nosedive. Many investors saw their investments evaporate. Companies that were once worth billions saw their valuations crumble. It was a rude awakening for those who had believed in the dot-com dream.

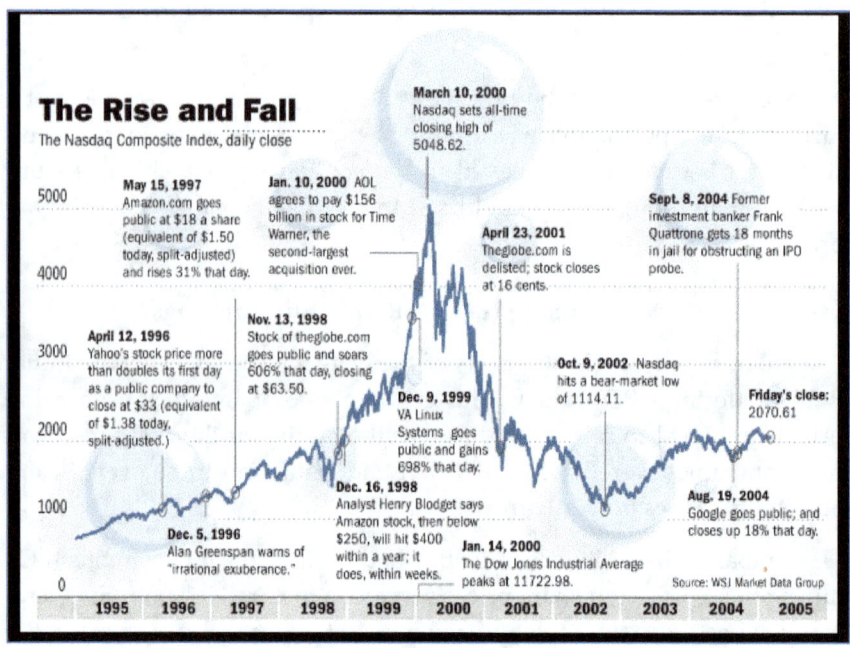

Figure 19 – Nasdaq Composite Index during Dot-Com bubble[17]

The Dot-Com Bubble left a significant mark on the world of finance and investing. It was a stark reminder of the dangers of speculative frenzies and the importance of examining the fundamentals of a company before investing in its stock.

The Survivors and Rise of Online Giants

Interestingly, while many dot-com companies did not survive the crash, some thrived. Amazon and eBay, for instance, emerged from the Dot-Com Bubble stronger and more resilient. These companies managed to adapt to changing market conditions and grow into the tech giants we know today.

Following the Dot-Com Bubble, new internet giants emerged, including Google and, later, Facebook. These companies learned from the mistakes of the dot-com era and built sustainable business models that withstood the test of time.

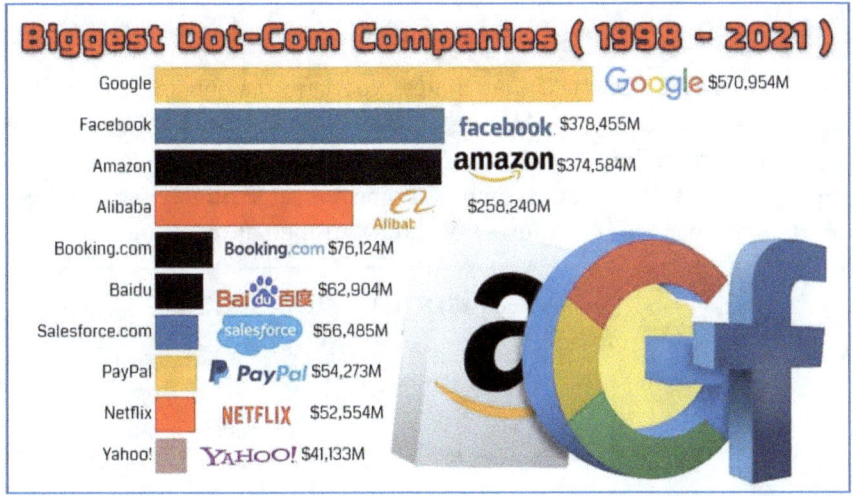

Figure 20 – Biggest Dot-Com Companies[18]

The Importance of Prudence: Diversification and Due Diligence

The Dot-Com Bubble serves as a lesson in the importance of prudence and caution in investing. It reminds us that markets can sometimes get carried away with excitement and that "get-rich-quick" dreams are often too good to be true. Diversifying investments and thoroughly researching companies are crucial strategies for avoiding the pitfalls of speculative bubbles.

While the Dot-Com Bubble had its share of excess and irrational exuberance, it was also a period of incredible innovation. The internet continued to transform the way we live, work, and communicate, with new online businesses and services continuously reshaping the world.

2.8. The Global Financial Crisis: The World on the Edge

Take a journey back to the late 2000s, a time when the world was shaken by a financial storm that affected people's lives, homes, and jobs. The Global Financial Crisis of 2007-2008 was one of the most significant economic events in modern history, and we're going to dive into this complex story in simpler terms to understand what happened and why.

The Housing Boom: Mortgages for All

In the early 2000s, the United States experienced a housing boom. That means lots of people were buying houses, and the prices of homes were going up and up. It seemed like a dream come true for many. People who never thought they could own a home were suddenly able to get mortgages (loans to buy houses), and they jumped at the chance.

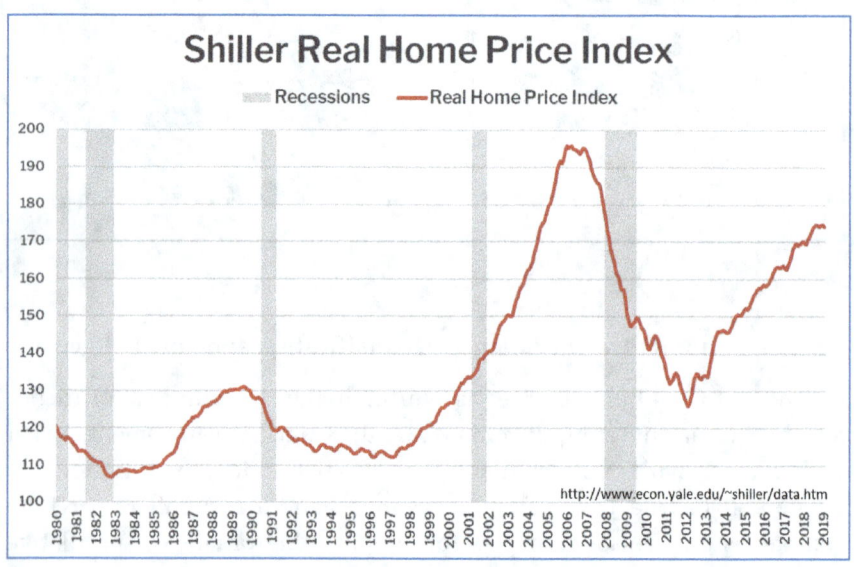

Figure 21 – Shiller Real Home Price Index during the housing bubble[19]

Banks and other lenders were eager to offer these mortgages because they believed the housing market was a safe bet. They gave out loans to people, even if they didn't have perfect credit. These loans often had low "teaser" interest rates, meaning the initial interest rate was low but would later go up.

The Risky Business of Subprime Mortgages

Some of these loans were known as "subprime mortgages." These were loans given to people with lower credit scores or those who didn't have a strong history of repaying debts. At first, it seemed like a good idea because it allowed more people to buy homes. But there was a problem.

The subprime mortgages had these teaser rates that would increase after a few years. Many people didn't fully understand the terms of their loans, and when the interest rates went up, they couldn't afford the higher payments. This led to a wave of home foreclosures, where people couldn't make their mortgage payments and lost their homes.

Figure 22 – For Sale houses during 2008[20]

The Financial Domino Effect: Toxic Assets

The troubles with subprime mortgages didn't just stop at the people who couldn't pay their loans. These mortgages were bundled together into complex financial products called mortgage-backed securities. These securities were sold to investors, including big financial institutions and even governments.

The problem was that these mortgage-backed securities contained a mix of good and bad loans. The bad loans were like poison mixed in with the good ones. When people started defaulting on their subprime mortgages, it caused the value of these securities to plummet. They became known as "toxic assets."

The Lehman Brothers Collapse: A Shockwave

One of the most significant moments in the Global Financial Crisis was the bankruptcy of Lehman Brothers in September 2008. Lehman Brothers was a big investment bank, and its collapse sent shockwaves through the financial system. It was like knocking over a domino in a long chain, and the effects were far-reaching.

Lehman Brothers' bankruptcy caused panic in the financial markets. It led to a loss of confidence in the stability of the entire banking system. People and institutions began to worry about the safety of their money, and there was a rush to withdraw funds from banks.

Figure 23 – Lehman Brothers closed during the global housing crisis[21]

Governments around the world realized they needed to take action to prevent a complete financial meltdown. The U.S. government implemented a series of emergency measures, including the Troubled Asset Relief Program (TARP). This program aimed to stabilize the financial system by injecting money into troubled banks.

Other governments also took steps to shore up their financial sectors. The crisis was not limited to the United States; it had become a global problem.

The Real Economy Hit Hard: Recession and Unemployment

The Global Financial Crisis wasn't just a problem for the financial industry. It had a real impact on the broader economy. Businesses struggled to access credit, and consumers cut back on spending. This led to a severe economic downturn, with unemployment rates rising as companies laid off workers.

People lost their homes, jobs, and savings. The crisis touched the lives of everyday individuals and caused tremendous hardship for many.

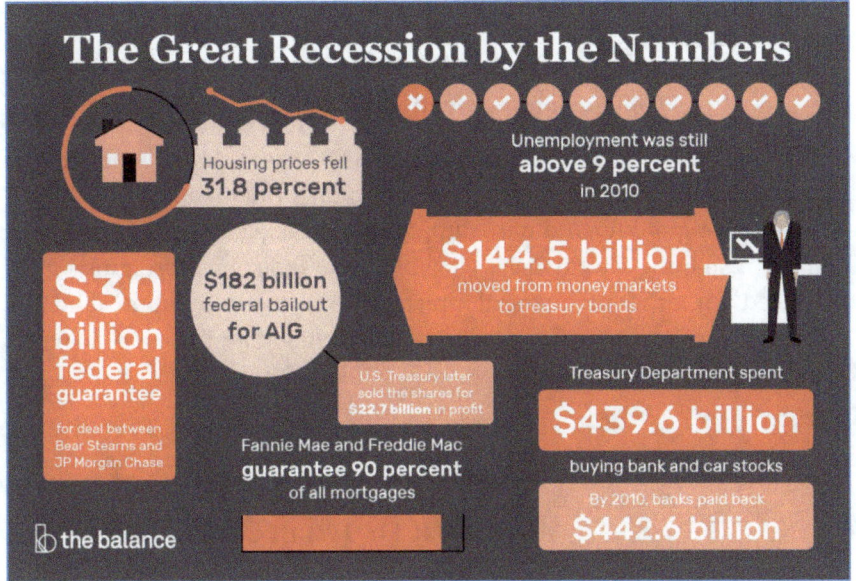

Figure 24 – The Great Recession by the Numbers[22]

Lessons Learned: The Importance of Responsible Lending and Regulation

The Global Financial Crisis taught us valuable lessons. It showed the dangers of reckless lending and the importance of responsible lending practices. It underscored the need for strong and effective financial regulation to prevent excessive risk-taking in the banking sector.

In the aftermath of the crisis, the United States implemented the Dodd-Frank Wall Street Reform and Consumer Protection Act. This legislation aimed to strengthen financial regulation, promote transparency, and prevent the excessive risk-taking that had contributed to the crisis.

The Role of Central Banks: Monetary Policy

Central banks, including the U.S. Federal Reserve, played a crucial role in responding to the crisis. They lowered interest rates and implemented monetary policies to stabilize the financial system and support economic recovery.

The Global Financial Crisis reshaped the financial landscape. It led to stricter regulations and oversight, and it prompted financial institutions to reevaluate their practices. It also left a lasting impact on the public's perception of the financial industry and reinforced the importance of financial stability.

Conclusion: Navigating the Seas of Finance

The Global Financial Crisis of 2007-2008 was a pivotal moment in history, a time when the world teetered on the brink of a financial abyss. While it brought pain and hardship, it also left a legacy of resilience and reform, reshaping the financial world for years to come. It reminds us of the need for prudent financial practices, effective regulation, and the importance of learning from the past as we navigate the ever-changing seas of finance.

2.9. The European Debt Crisis: A Continent in Trouble

Imagine a continent where countries share the same currency, the euro, and work together as part of the European Union (EU). But in the early 2010s, this dream of unity turned into a nightmare. The European Debt Crisis, also known as the Eurozone Crisis, plunged many countries into financial turmoil, causing widespread uncertainty and challenges. Let's explore this complex crisis in simpler terms to understand what happened and why.

The Euro: A Shared Currency

The euro is like a shared piggy bank for many countries in Europe. They use it as their official currency, and it helps them trade with one another. The idea was to make things easier and strengthen their economies by working together.

The early 2000s, when the euro was introduced, was an exciting time. It seemed like a great idea for countries to use the same currency, as it would simplify trade and make it easier for people to travel and do business across borders.

Figure 25 – Picture of 100 Euro[23]

However, some countries didn't manage their finances as well as others. They spent more money than they had and borrowed a lot. This behavior created problems down the road.

The Real Estate Bubble: Easy Money and Overborrowing

One of the major issues was a real estate bubble in some countries, like Spain and Ireland. A real estate bubble is when the prices of houses and properties soar too high, too fast. People thought the value of their homes would keep going up, so they borrowed a lot of money to buy properties, often using mortgages.

Banks in these countries made it easy to borrow, and people took on big mortgages. But when the bubble burst, the value of their homes plummeted, leaving many homeowners owing more than their homes were worth.

The Debt Crisis Begins: Greece Takes the Spotlight

Greece was one of the first countries to face serious problems during the European Debt Crisis. The Greek government had borrowed a lot of money and couldn't pay it back. They had run up a massive debt.

When Greece couldn't pay its bills, it created a ripple effect. People worried that other countries might also have trouble with their debts. Investors became nervous and started demanding higher interest rates to lend money to those countries. This made it even harder for countries to manage their debts.

The Domino Effect: Contagion Spreads

As the crisis unfolded, it spread to other countries, including Portugal, Ireland, Italy, and Spain, often referred to as the "PIIGS." These countries faced similar debt problems, and their economies suffered.

	Italy	Spain	Portugal	Ireland	Greece
■ UK bank exposure	£45bn	£70bn	£15bn	£88bn	£8bn
■ Debt to GDP	118.3%	63.5%	81.3%	93.6%	130.2%

Figure 26 - European Debt Crisis Debt Levels[24]

The crisis wasn't just about the debt itself. It was also about the fear and uncertainty surrounding the situation. Investors became cautious about lending money to governments, which made it more expensive for these countries to borrow. The rising interest rates put even more pressure on their budgets.

To help some of the struggling countries, the European Union and the International Monetary Fund (IMF) stepped in with bailout packages. These were like emergency loans, but they came with conditions. The countries receiving the bailouts had to implement austerity measures, which meant making deep budget cuts and economic reforms.

Austerity was a tough pill to swallow for many people in these countries. It meant reduced government spending, job cuts, and sometimes even reduced wages. People protested, and there was a lot of anger and frustration.

The European Central Bank Steps In

The European Central Bank (ECB) played a significant role in trying to stabilize the situation. It started buying government bonds from struggling countries to help lower their borrowing costs. The ECB also implemented policies to support the financial system.

The crisis continued to affect more countries, including Cyprus, which faced its own set of financial troubles. Cyprus needed a bailout, too, and it was a stark reminder of the ongoing challenges.

Recovering from the European Debt Crisis was a slow and challenging process. Many of the affected countries had to make difficult economic and fiscal changes. Some made progress, but the scars of the crisis remained.

Lessons Learned: The Importance of Responsible Financial Management

The European Debt Crisis taught us some important lessons. It highlighted the need for responsible financial management by governments and the importance of keeping an eye on debts. It also emphasized the importance of having a plan for tough times.

The euro is still the shared currency of many European countries. While the European Debt Crisis is behind us, challenges remain. It's an ongoing journey of finding ways to make the euro work for everyone while also preventing similar crises from happening again.

Conclusion: Weathering the Storms of Finance

The European Debt Crisis was a trying time for many countries in Europe. It taught us about the complexities of shared currencies and the importance of sound financial management. While the crisis was a tough period, it also brought forth important lessons and underscored the resilience of nations in the face of financial challenges. As Europe continues to navigate the ever-changing seas of finance, the legacy of this crisis reminds us of the need for vigilance and cooperation in an interconnected world.

2.10. The Flash Crash of 2010: The Day the Market Went Wild

Picture this: You're watching the stock market, and suddenly, in a matter of minutes, prices of major companies' shares go haywire. Some stocks that were worth a lot drop to just a penny and then bounce back up. It's chaos, confusion, and panic. This is the story of the Flash Crash of 2010, a strange and unsettling event in the world of finance.

The Stock Market: Where Prices Meet

The stock market is like a big marketplace where people buy and sell tiny pieces of ownership in companies. These tiny pieces are called "shares" or "stocks." The prices of these shares go up and down, depending on how well people think the companies are doing and how much they're willing to pay for the shares.

On May 6, 2010, something bizarre happened. The stock market went on a roller coaster ride like never before. Within minutes, prices of many well-known stocks dropped dramatically and then rebounded. Some stocks went from their normal prices to just a few cents and then back to their original values. It was like watching a heart monitor jump up and down.

At the heart of the Flash Crash was fear and panic. Some believe that the trouble started when a big trader used a computer program to sell a massive amount of futures contracts. Futures contracts are agreements to buy or sell something (in this case, stocks) at a specific price on a future date.

The problem was that this massive sale created a wave of panic among other traders. They saw the prices plummeting, and they started selling their stocks too. The panic spread like wildfire through the stock market.

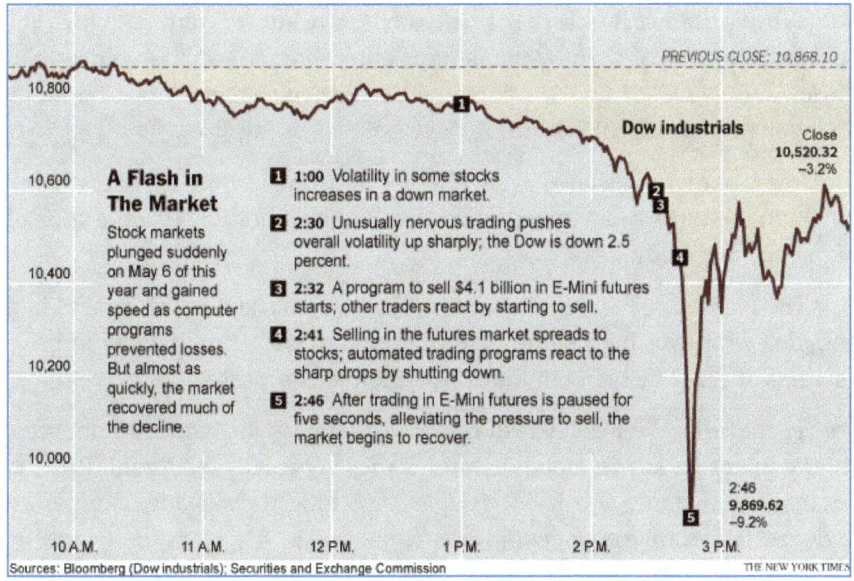

Figure 27 – A Flash in the market[25]

Algo Trading: The Rise of Machines

Part of the issue was the increasing use of computer programs for trading. These programs, called "algorithms" or "algos," can buy and sell stocks automatically based on certain conditions. They're like little robots that make trading decisions.

These algorithms can work very quickly, much faster than humans. But in the Flash Crash, they might have worked too fast. Some algorithms may have reacted to the falling prices by selling even more, which worsened the situation.

Figure 28 – Algo Trading by years[26]

During the Flash Crash, the prices of many stocks went haywire. For example, shares of Disney, the famous entertainment company, dropped from about $40 to just a penny before bouncing back up. The same happened to shares of Accenture, a global consulting firm.

Imagine owning shares of a well-known company worth $40 each, and then, in the blink of an eye, they're worth almost nothing. It's the stuff of financial nightmares.

The Flash Crash created chaos in the stock market. Some traders had no idea what was happening. They couldn't make sense of the wild price swings. It was like being in a storm without a compass.

Thankfully, the Flash Crash didn't last long. In just about 30 minutes, stock prices began to stabilize, and things returned to normal. But the damage was done, and it left people scratching their heads, wondering how such a strange event could occur.

Investigations and Reforms: Seeking Answers

After the Flash Crash, investigations were conducted to figure out what went wrong. Regulators and experts analyzed the data to understand the causes. They identified the need for more safeguards to prevent such rapid and severe price swings in the future.

One response to the Flash Crash was the introduction of "circuit breakers." These are like pause buttons for the stock market. If prices swing too wildly, the circuit breakers can temporarily halt trading. This gives everyone a chance to catch their breath and prevents further chaos.

The Flash Crash also raised questions about high-frequency trading. This is when traders use super-fast computers and algorithms to buy and sell stocks in the blink of an eye. Some argued that high-frequency trading contributed to the chaos.

Lessons Learned: Technology and Caution

The Flash Crash of 2010 taught us a few important lessons. It showed us the power of technology in today's stock markets, where computers and algorithms play a significant role. It also highlighted the need for safeguards to prevent rapid and extreme price swings.

The Flash Crash was like a speed bump in the world of finance. It was a moment of confusion and chaos, but it also spurred important discussions about how to make our financial markets safer and more stable. As we continue to navigate the ever-evolving landscape of finance, the lessons from the Flash Crash remind us to balance technology with caution and vigilance.

2.11. Cryptocurrency Market Crashes: Roller Coasters of the Digital World

Welcome to the world of cryptocurrencies, where digital coins and tokens are changing the way we think about money. But just like any roller coaster, the cryptocurrency market has seen its share of thrilling highs and stomach-churning lows. We're about to dive into the world of Cryptocurrency Market Crashes in simpler terms to understand what happened and why.

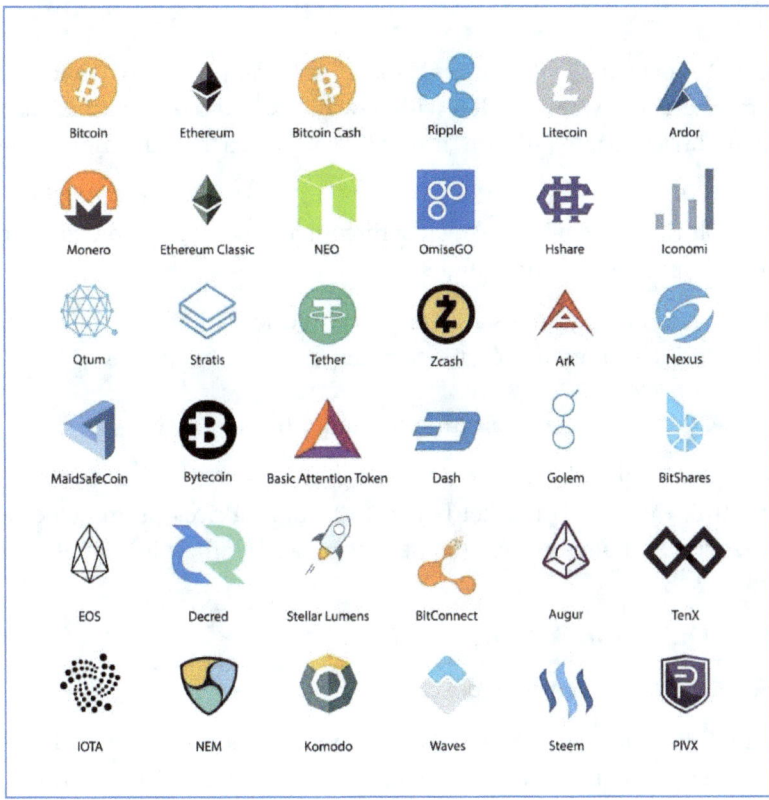

Figure 29 – Different Cryptocurrencies[27]

The Birth of Cryptocurrencies: Bitcoin and Beyond

Cryptocurrencies started with Bitcoin. Imagine Bitcoin as a digital version of money. You can't hold it in your hand, but it's stored on a computer as lines of code. Bitcoin, and later other cryptocurrencies, became popular because they promised to be secure, decentralized, and free from traditional banks and governments.

People were excited about the potential of this new way of handling money. They saw it as a form of digital gold, a new kind of investment, and a way to make quick profits.

Crypto Mania: The Hype Train Takes Off

Around 2017, cryptocurrencies like Bitcoin, Ethereum, and many others started gaining a lot of attention. Prices were going up, and everyone wanted to jump on the crypto train. People were hearing stories about those who had bought a few Bitcoins years earlier and were now millionaires.

Crypto exchanges (websites where you can buy, sell, and trade cryptocurrencies) were flooded with new users, and the market seemed to be on an unstoppable bull run. It was like a gold rush of the digital age.

In late 2017, the price of Bitcoin soared to nearly $20,000 per coin. This was a historic high, and it wasn't just Bitcoin; many other cryptocurrencies were reaching their all-time highs, too.

People who had invested early were celebrating their newfound wealth, and it seemed like cryptocurrencies were unstoppable.

The Beginning of the End: The Crash

But just as quickly as prices went up, they started coming down. In early 2018, the crypto market began to tumble. Prices plummeted, and people who had bought in at the peak were seeing their investments lose value.

Why Did the Market Crash?

Several factors contributed to the crash:

1. **Regulatory Concerns:** Governments around the world began expressing concerns about the unregulated nature of cryptocurrencies. They were worried about things like fraud and

money laundering. Some countries even started talking about banning or heavily regulating cryptocurrencies.

2. **Speculation and Hype:** Many people bought cryptocurrencies not because they understood the technology or the projects behind them but because they thought prices would keep going up. When prices started falling, panic selling began.

3. **Security Breaches:** Crypto exchanges, where people stored and traded their digital assets, were vulnerable to cyberattacks. Some high-profile hacks resulted in the theft of significant amounts of cryptocurrencies, eroding trust in the safety of these platforms.

4. **Lack of Real-World Use:** At the time, cryptocurrencies were not widely used for everyday transactions. They were more like speculative assets, and the lack of real-world adoption raised questions about their long-term value.

The Aftermath: HODL and Recovery

In the midst of the crash, a popular phrase emerged in the crypto community: "HODL." It was a misspelling of "hold," and it became a meme. The idea was that instead of panicking and selling during market downturns, you should "hodl" your coins and wait for the market to recover.

Figure 30 – HODL meme[28]

Over time, the market did start to recover, and some cryptocurrencies regained value. However, not all of them did, and many people who had bought at the peak of the hype ended up with losses.

One aspect of the crypto market that contributed to the crash was the Initial Coin Offering (ICO) craze. ICOs were like crowdfunding campaigns where new cryptocurrencies were launched, and people could buy them at an early stage. The problem was that many of these projects turned out to be scams or never delivered on their promises.

Investors poured money into these ICOs, hoping to get rich quickly. When many of these projects failed, it led to a loss of trust in the market and contributed to the crash.

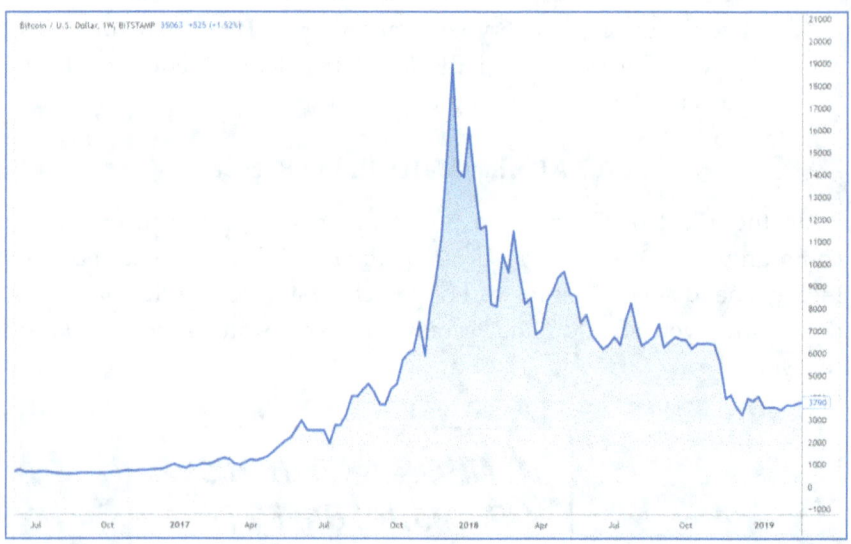

Figure 31 – Bitcoin Price Chart. Built by the Author using TradingView

Lessons Learned: Volatility and Caution

The Cryptocurrency Market Crashes of 2018 taught us some important lessons. Cryptocurrencies are incredibly volatile, and their prices can swing wildly in a short time. It's also essential to be cautious and do your research when investing in this space. Just because something is new and exciting doesn't mean it's a guaranteed path to riches.

The world of cryptocurrencies continues to evolve. Since the crash of 2018, we've seen more regulation, increased adoption of blockchain technology (the underlying tech of cryptocurrencies), and the rise of stablecoins (cryptocurrencies designed to have stable values).

Cryptocurrencies are still around, and the market continues to have its ups and downs. Some people have made fortunes, while others have seen their investments disappear. It's a world of risk and reward, and it's always changing.

While Bitcoin remains the most well-known cryptocurrency, many other digital coins and tokens, known as "altcoins," have entered the scene. These altcoins have diverse features and purposes, from enhancing privacy and security to enabling smart contracts and decentralized applications.

The Evolution of Use Cases: Real-World Adoption

One of the significant developments in the cryptocurrency space has been the increased adoption of real-world use cases. Cryptocurrencies are no longer just speculative assets; they are being integrated into various industries. Some companies accept cryptocurrencies as payment, and there are even crypto-based debit cards.

#	Coin		Price	1h	24h	7d	24h Volume	Mkt Cap	Last 7 Days
☆ 1	Bitcoin BTC	Buy	$35,055.78	-0.1%	0.8%	1.3%	$11,971,497,757	$684,079,937,800	
☆ 2	Ethereum ETH	Buy	$1,892.36	-0.3%	3.0%	5.4%	$12,935,796,376	$227,251,508,326	
☆ 3	Tether USDT		$1.00	-0.1%	0.0%	0.0%	$25,037,066,737	$85,383,721,509	
☆ 4	BNB BNB	Buy	$244.17	0.1%	3.4%	7.4%	$542,093,179	$37,487,378,753	
☆ 5	XRP XRP	Buy	$0.656116	0.2%	7.0%	17.5%	$1,455,111,933	$35,237,158,470	
☆ 6	USDC USDC		$0.999948	0.0%	-0.0%	0.0%	$5,313,753,413	$24,573,173,745	
☆ 7	Solana SOL	Buy	$40.99	-0.1%	-1.6%	23.9%	$906,344,098	$17,198,971,508	
☆ 8	Lido Staked Ether STETH		$1,892.14	-0.3%	3.0%	5.5%	$6,588,582	$16,818,001,645	
☆ 9	Cardano ADA	Buy	$0.346374	-0.3%	6.8%	18.5%	$303,185,576	$12,068,983,555	
☆ 10	Dogecoin DOGE	Buy	$0.071279	0.1%	4.2%	2.3%	$527,780,801	$10,057,910,601	

Figure 32 - Cryptocurrency Prices by Market Cap[29]

The cryptocurrency space still faces challenges. Governments and regulators continue to grapple with how to oversee this new digital frontier. Security remains a concern, as hacks and scams are a constant threat. Investors need to be cautious and ensure they store their digital assets securely.

Conclusion: Riding the Crypto Waves

The cryptocurrency market crash of 2018 was like a storm in the world of digital money. They were a reminder of the extreme volatility and the speculative nature of the crypto market. As we continue to explore the world of cryptocurrencies, the lessons from the crash encourage us to be cautious, do our research, and approach this digital frontier with eyes wide open. The cryptocurrency roller coaster continues, with its ups and downs, and it's a ride that's not over yet.

2.12. The COVID-19 Stock Market Crash: When the World Got Sick, and So Did the Economy

Imagine a world facing an invisible enemy, a virus called COVID-19. As it spread rapidly, it not only affected people's health but also caused a severe shock to the world's financial systems. The COVID-19 Stock Market Crash of 2020 was like a massive earthquake in the world of finance. Let's dive into this complex event in simpler terms to understand what happened and why.

The Stock Market: Where Companies Go Public

First, let's recap what the stock market is. It's like a marketplace where companies can go public. This means they sell tiny pieces of ownership, called shares or stocks, to people who want to invest in the company's success.

When a company does well, its stock prices go up, and investors make money. But when things go wrong, stock prices can drop, and investors lose money.

The Start of the Crisis: COVID-19 Arrives

In late 2019 and early 2020, a new virus called COVID-19, or simply "coronavirus," began to spread. It caused a disease that made people very sick, especially those who were older or had health problems.

Countries around the world tried to contain the virus by imposing restrictions. They closed businesses, stopped people from traveling, and encouraged everyone to stay at home. These measures were taken to protect public health.

The restrictions had a big impact on businesses. Many companies had to close their doors, and people lost their jobs. It was like a giant pause button had been pressed on the economy. With businesses not operating, their profits started to drop.

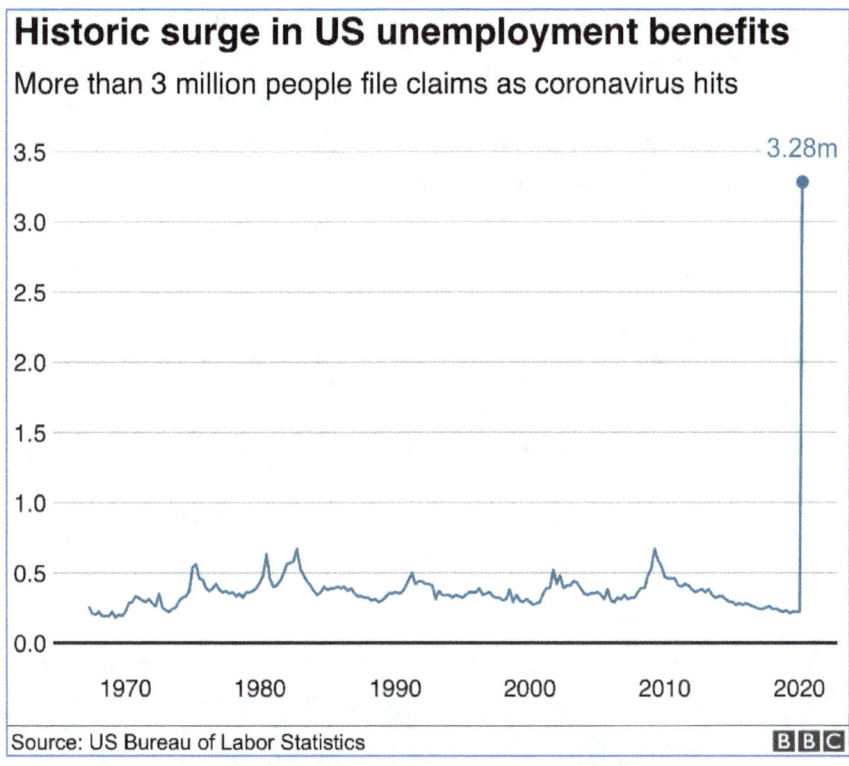

Historic surge in US unemployment benefits
More than 3 million people file claims as coronavirus hits

Figure 33 – Unemployment Rate during 2020.[30]

The stock market, where people buy and sell stocks, began to react to the growing economic uncertainty. Investors became worried about the impact of the virus on businesses and the overall economy. As a result, stock prices started to fall.

The Black Swan: Unpredictable and Rare

The COVID-19 Stock Market Crash was often referred to as a "Black Swan" event. A Black Swan is something extremely rare and unpredictable. It's like a black swan appearing in a place where only white swans are expected.

This term is used in finance to describe an event that catches everyone by surprise. The COVID-19 pandemic was a Black Swan, as no one could have predicted such a global health crisis.

During the COVID-19 Stock Market Crash, we saw extreme volatility. This means that stock prices were swinging wildly. One day, they would go down a lot, and the next day, they might bounce back up. It was a roller coaster ride for investors.

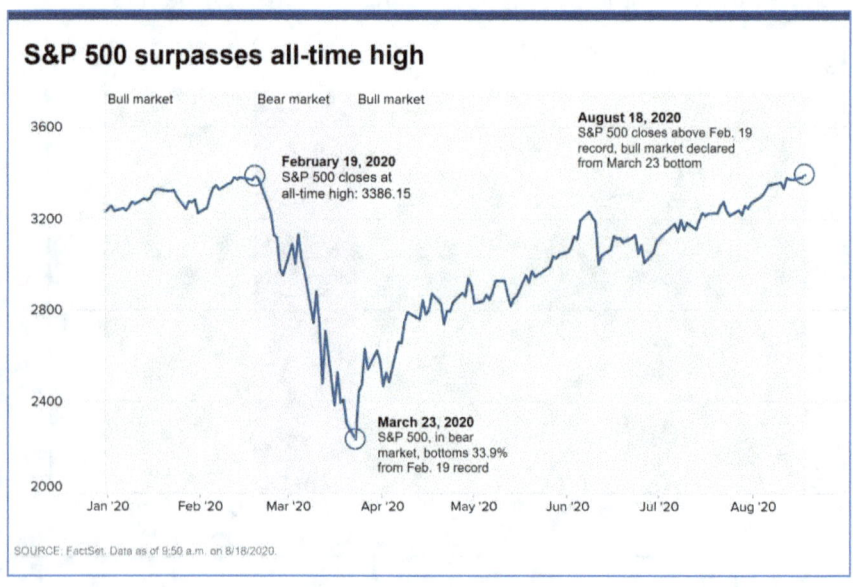

Figure 34 – Stock Market during the Coronavirus pandemic[31]

Investor Behavior: Fear and Uncertainty

The crash was driven by a lot of fear and uncertainty. Investors were worried about the future. They didn't know when the pandemic would end, and they didn't know how much damage it would do to businesses.

When investors are uncertain and afraid, they often sell their stocks, which pushes prices down even further. This creates a vicious cycle that can lead to a market crash.

Government Responses: Stimulus and Support

Governments around the world took action to try to prevent the economy from collapsing. They introduced stimulus packages, which were like financial boosts to help individuals and businesses during the tough times.

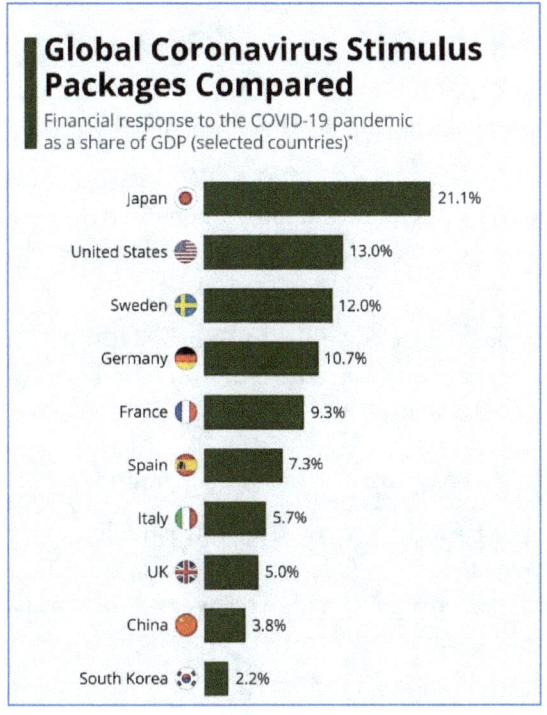

Figure 35 – Global Coronavirus stimulus as % of GDP[32]

Central banks, like the U.S. Federal Reserve, lowered interest rates to make borrowing cheaper. They also took other measures to keep the financial system stable.

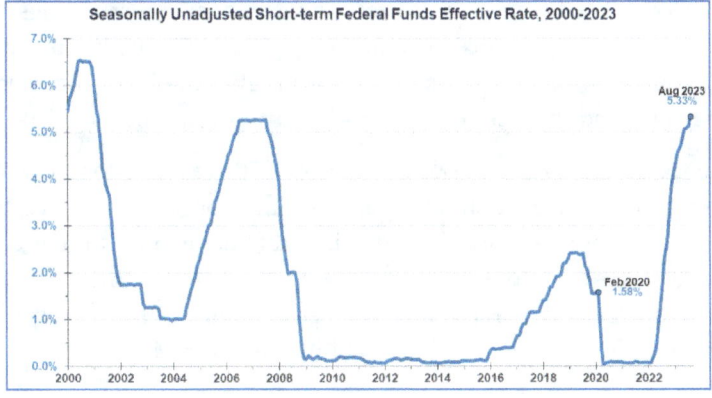

Figure 36 – Short-Term Federal Funds Rate[33]

Some industries were hit particularly hard by the pandemic and the resulting economic downturn. Travel and tourism businesses, such as airlines and hotels, saw their revenues plummet as people stopped traveling.

Restaurants and entertainment venues had to close, causing job losses and financial hardship for many. These industries were among the most affected by the crisis.

On the other hand, some industries benefited from the pandemic. Technology companies and e-commerce businesses thrived as people turned to online shopping and remote work.

Tech giants like Amazon, Apple, and Microsoft saw their stock prices rise during the crisis. They played a crucial role in keeping the economy moving during lockdowns.

The Long Road to Recovery: Gradual Healing

The COVID-19 Stock Market Crash wasn't like a typical market downturn. It was tied to a global health crisis, and that made it more complex. While stock prices started to recover as the world adapted to the new reality, it was a slow and uncertain process.

One key turning point was the development and distribution of COVID-19 vaccines. As vaccines became more widely available, there was hope that the world could return to a semblance of normalcy. This hope had a positive impact on investor sentiment.

Lessons Learned: Resilience and Preparation

The COVID-19 Stock Market Crash taught us several crucial lessons. It underscored the importance of being prepared for the unexpected and the need for resilient financial systems. It also highlighted the importance of public health and the role of government support in times of crisis.

The COVID-19 Stock Market Crash of 2020 was a historic chapter in the world of finance. It showed us how interconnected the world has become and how a global health crisis can have profound economic consequences. As we continue to navigate the ever-changing landscape of finance, the lessons from this crisis remind us of the importance of resilience, preparedness, and the ability to adapt in the face of the unexpected.

3. Lessons and Takeaways from Financial Crashes

Financial crashes, whether caused by economic turmoil, market speculation, or unexpected events, have left their mark on history. These events have often resulted in economic hardships, personal suffering, and significant losses for investors. While each financial crash is unique in its own way, there are common lessons and takeaways that can help individuals, governments, and the financial industry navigate future challenges.

In this chapter, we'll explore these lessons and takeaways in simpler terms to better understand how we can learn from the past.

1. Financial Literacy Matters

Lesson: Understanding how money, investments, and the financial system work is crucial for everyone. It empowers individuals to make informed decisions and avoid financial pitfalls.

Takeaway: Invest time in learning about personal finance, saving, investing, and how the financial system operates. There are many resources available, from books to online courses, that can help you become financially literate.

Financial literacy is like having a map to navigate the world of money. When you understand basic concepts like budgeting, saving, and investing, you're better equipped to make wise financial decisions. Think of it as learning to read the signs on the road to financial success. Without financial literacy, you might get lost or make costly wrong turns.

2. Diversify Your Investments

Lesson: Putting all your eggs in one basket is risky. When you diversify your investments, you spread the risk and can better weather market downturns.

Takeaway: Don't put all your money in a single investment or asset class. Diversify your portfolio by investing in a mix of stocks, bonds, real estate, and other assets.

Diversification is like having a variety of foods in your diet. You wouldn't eat the same thing every day because it might not provide all the nutrients you need. Similarly, diversifying your investments helps spread risk and can protect your finances during turbulent times.

3. Beware of Speculation

Lesson: Speculation, or making investments based on the hope of making quick profits, can lead to significant losses. It's like gambling with your money.

Takeaway: Invest for the long term and avoid getting caught up in market frenzies. Make informed decisions based on research and a clear investment strategy.

Speculation is like playing roulette in a casino. You might win big, but the odds are against you. Investing with a clear plan and a focus on long-term goals is like making wise choices that lead to financial security and success.

4. Plan for the Unexpected

Lesson: Unexpected events, whether natural disasters, health crises, or other emergencies, can have a profound impact on the economy and financial markets.

Takeaway: Build an emergency fund to cover essential expenses in case of unexpected disruptions. Have insurance to protect against risks you can't predict.

Planning for the unexpected is like packing an umbrella when you leave the house. You hope you won't need it, but if a sudden rainstorm hits, you're prepared. Similarly, having an emergency fund and insurance can provide a safety net when life's unexpected challenges come your way.

5. Government Intervention Can Stabilize Markets

Lesson: During financial crises, governments can play a vital role in stabilizing the economy and financial markets through policies and stimulus measures.

Takeaway: Understand the role of government in the economy. Government interventions can help prevent a crisis from becoming even more severe.

Government intervention is like the safety nets at a circus trapeze act. They're there to catch you if you fall. In the financial world, governments can use policies and stimulus measures to prevent an economic crash from becoming a full-blown catastrophe.

6. Avoid Overleveraging

Lesson: Borrowing too much money to invest can magnify losses in a market downturn. It's like walking a financial tightrope.

Takeaway: Be cautious when using leverage (borrowed money) for investments. Avoid overextending yourself financially.

Overleveraging is like stacking too many plates on a wobbly tower. When one plate falls, it can bring the whole tower crashing down. It's important to balance borrowing with financial stability to avoid a precarious situation.

7. Stay Informed and Adaptive

Lesson: The financial world is always changing. Staying informed about market trends, economic conditions, and emerging risks is essential.

Takeaway: Keep yourself updated with financial news and trends. Be ready to adapt your investment strategy as circumstances change.

Staying informed is like using a GPS to navigate unfamiliar terrain. It provides you with real-time information and helps you make decisions based on the current landscape. In the financial world, adaptability and staying informed are like having a GPS for your investments.

8. Emotions Play a Role

Lesson: Emotions like fear and greed can lead to impulsive investment decisions. This behavior can harm your financial well-being.

Takeaway: Recognize the role of emotions in your financial decisions. Avoid impulsive actions and stick to a well-thought-out plan.

Emotions are like the wind that can push you off course when sailing. They can make you deviate from your planned route and lead to stormy financial seas. Staying calm and rational is like having a steady hand on the financial tiller, keeping you on course.

9. Prioritize Long-Term Goals

Lesson: Short-term market fluctuations are part of investing. Focusing on long-term financial goals can help you weather these ups and downs.

Takeaway: Set clear long-term financial goals and create an investment plan that aligns with those objectives.

Long-term goals are like a distant destination on a road trip. You might encounter detours and traffic along the way, but you stay on track because you know where you want to go. Similarly, having long-term financial goals helps you stay focused and patient during market ups and downs.

10. Balance Risk and Reward

Lesson: High returns often come with higher risk. It's essential to find a balance that suits your financial situation and goals.

Takeaway: Assess your risk tolerance and create an investment portfolio that matches your comfort level with risk.

Balancing risk and reward is like choosing the right gear for a hike. You wouldn't wear heavy winter clothing on a summer hike, and you wouldn't wear shorts in freezing weather. Similarly, assessing your risk tolerance and creating an investment portfolio that matches your comfort level is like choosing the right gear for your financial journey.

11. Seek Professional Advice When Needed

Lesson: There are financial experts and advisors who can help you make informed decisions, especially during complex financial crises.

Takeaway: If you're unsure about your financial strategy or investments, seek professional guidance from a financial advisor.

Seeking professional advice is like consulting a travel guide when exploring a foreign country. They know the terrain, can recommend the best places to visit, and help you avoid pitfalls. Similarly, a financial advisor can provide guidance and expertise to navigate the complex world of investments.

12. Learn from History

Lesson: History can be a valuable teacher. By studying past financial crashes, we can better understand the patterns and factors that contribute to these events.

Takeaway: Explore the history of financial crashes to gain insights into what went wrong and how to avoid similar mistakes in the future.

Learning from history is like reading a treasure map. It can lead you to hidden knowledge and valuable lessons. Similarly, studying past financial crashes can provide insights into the factors that contributed to these events, helping you avoid similar mistakes in the future.

13. Understand the Impact of Economic Policies

Lesson: Economic policies, such as monetary and fiscal measures, can have a significant impact on financial stability.

Takeaway: Be aware of how government policies can influence the economy and financial markets. This understanding can guide your financial decisions.

Understanding economic policies is like having a compass in a dense forest. It helps you navigate and make informed decisions. In the financial world, being aware of how government policies influence the economy and markets can guide your financial choices and keep you on course.

14. Collaboration and Cooperation Are Vital

Lesson: In times of crisis, working together is crucial. Governments, businesses, and individuals must collaborate to overcome financial challenges.

Takeaway: Recognize the importance of cooperation and collective efforts to address financial crises effectively.

Collaboration and cooperation are like a team rowing a boat in a storm. When everyone works together and follows the same rhythm, they can navigate even the roughest waters. Similarly, during financial crises, cooperation among governments, businesses, and individuals is essential to overcoming challenges and stabilizing the financial ship.

15. Stay Patient and Persistent

Lesson: Recovering from a financial crash often takes time. Patience and persistence are key to rebuilding and moving forward.

Takeaway: Be patient during difficult financial periods. Stay persistent in working toward your long-term goals.

Patience and persistence are like taking one step at a time on a long journey. It may seem slow, but each step brings you closer to your destination. Similarly, during financial crises, being patient and persistent helps you recover and work toward your long-term financial goals.

Conclusion: Navigating the Financial Landscape

Financial crashes have left indelible marks on history, but they also offer valuable lessons and takeaways. By understanding these lessons and implementing the corresponding takeaways, individuals, and governments can better prepare for future challenges and navigate the ever-changing financial landscape with confidence and resilience. Whether you're a seasoned investor or just beginning your financial journey, these lessons can serve as a guiding light in the world of finance. Remember, just like a well-equipped traveler, being prepared and informed can help you navigate the twists and turns of the financial landscape and reach your destination with confidence.

4. Future Challenges in Finance: Navigating Tomorrow's Waters

As we sail through the sea of finance, it's essential to keep an eye on the horizon and anticipate the challenges that lie ahead. The world of money and investments is always evolving, and being prepared for future challenges is crucial. In this chapter, we'll explore the potential challenges and changes that may shape the financial landscape in the coming years, using simple words to understand what the future might hold.

1. Technological Transformations

Challenge: Technology is constantly changing the way we handle money and investments. From digital currencies to artificial intelligence-driven trading, the financial world is undergoing a technological revolution.

Anticipation: Stay up to date with the latest financial technology (FinTech) trends. Be prepared to adapt to new ways of managing money and investing, and understand the potential benefits and risks.

Imagine technology as a wind that powers your financial sailboat. It can push you forward, but you need to know how to harness it. Staying informed about new financial technologies and being ready to embrace them can help you sail smoothly in the tech-driven financial seas.

2. Climate Change and Sustainability

Challenge: Climate change is impacting the world, and it has significant implications for the financial sector. Sustainable and responsible investing is becoming more critical as investors consider environmental, social, and governance (ESG) factors.

Anticipation: Educate yourself about ESG investing and its impact on financial markets. Consider sustainable and responsible investment options that align with your values and financial goals.

Climate change is like a wave rising in the financial sea. It can impact businesses, investments, and even the stability of financial markets. By choosing sustainable and responsible investments, you can be part of the solution to address this challenge.

3. Global Economic Uncertainty

Challenge: The global economy is always changing. Trade tensions, geopolitical conflicts, and unforeseen events like health crises can create economic uncertainties that affect investments and financial stability.

Anticipation: Diversify your investments and stay informed about global economic trends. Being prepared for economic ups and downs can help you navigate uncertain waters.

Global economic uncertainty is like unpredictable weather at sea. By diversifying your financial portfolio and staying informed about global economic trends, you can better prepare for the economic winds that may come your way.

4. Retirement Planning

Challenge: As life expectancy increases and traditional pension systems evolve, retirement planning is becoming more critical. Many people face the challenge of ensuring they have enough money to support their retirement years.

Anticipation: Start planning for retirement early and consider saving and investing for your future. Understand different retirement account options and explore ways to secure your financial future.

Retirement planning is like charting a course for your financial future. By starting early and setting aside money for your retirement, you can ensure a comfortable and secure journey during your golden years.

5. Regulatory Changes

Challenge: Governments and financial regulators can introduce new rules and regulations that impact the financial industry. Understanding and complying with these changes is essential.

Anticipation: Stay informed about financial regulations and be ready to adapt to new rules. Consulting with financial advisors or experts can help you navigate regulatory changes effectively.

Regulatory changes are like updates to the rules of the financial game. By staying informed and adapting to new regulations, you can continue to play the financial game with confidence and adherence to the rules.

6. Income Inequality

Challenge: Income inequality is a growing concern, and it can have consequences for the economy and financial markets. Addressing this challenge involves finding ways to reduce the wealth gap.

Anticipation: Consider the impact of income inequality on your financial decisions. Support policies and investments that contribute to a more equitable and inclusive financial system.

Income inequality is like a turbulent sea that can create waves of financial instability. By supporting policies and investments that promote economic equity, you can contribute to a more stable and fair financial environment.

7. Demographic Shifts

Challenge: Changing demographics, such as an aging population and shifts in workforce dynamics, can influence financial markets and retirement planning.

Anticipation: Be aware of demographic shifts and consider their impact on your financial situation. Adjust your financial plans to account for changing demographics, such as longer life expectancies.

Demographic shifts are like currents in the financial sea. They can influence the direction and speed of your financial journey. By understanding these shifts and adjusting your plans accordingly, you can navigate the waters with confidence.

8. Cybersecurity Threats

Challenge: With increasing reliance on digital systems, the financial sector is vulnerable to cyberattacks. Protecting your financial information and investments from online threats is crucial.

Anticipation: Invest in strong cybersecurity measures, such as secure passwords and two-factor authentication. Stay vigilant about protecting your online financial accounts and personal information.

Cybersecurity threats are like pirates in the digital ocean, trying to steal your financial treasure. By taking measures to protect your online financial accounts and information, you can safeguard your financial ship from these modern-day pirates.

9. Healthcare Costs

Challenge: Healthcare costs are rising, and they can have a significant impact on personal finances. Preparing for unexpected medical expenses is essential.

Anticipation: Consider healthcare costs in your financial planning. Invest in health insurance and build an emergency fund to cover unexpected medical bills.

Healthcare costs are like unpredictable waves that can capsize your financial boat. By preparing for these costs through health insurance and emergency funds, you can ensure a smoother financial voyage, even in stormy medical seas.

10. Evolving Investment Options

Challenge: The landscape of investment options is always changing. From cryptocurrencies to innovative startups, new investment opportunities can be enticing but also risky.

Anticipation: Educate yourself about new investment options and consider their potential risks and rewards. Diversify your investments wisely, balancing traditional and innovative options.

Evolving investment options are like new islands appearing on the financial horizon. They offer opportunities, but you need to explore them cautiously. By staying informed and diversifying wisely, you can safely navigate the ever-changing world of investments.

The future of finance holds both challenges and opportunities. By being aware of these potential challenges and preparing for them, you can navigate the financial waters with confidence. Just as a skilled sailor knows the importance of reading the wind and adjusting the sails, you can adapt to the changing financial landscape, making informed decisions to secure your financial journey. Remember that the skills you gain in anticipation of these challenges are like a sturdy rudder, helping you steer your financial ship toward a successful and secure destination.

5. Conclusion and What Shall You Do Now

As we prepare to anchor our journey through the financial world, remember that the seas of finance are vast and ever-changing. The stories of crashes, lessons learned, and future challenges have equipped you with valuable knowledge and insights.

Just as skilled sailors set out with the wind in their sails and a map to guide them, you now have a compass for your financial voyage. Whether you're a novice setting sail for the first time or an experienced captain navigating the financial waters, these principles will serve as your guiding star.

Financial literacy is your North Star, ensuring you understand the language of money. Diversification is your lifeboat, keeping your investments afloat in turbulent times. Avoiding speculation is your steady course, leading to long-term financial success. Preparing for the unexpected is your safety net, providing security in times of trouble. Government support is your rescue raft when economic storms hit. Avoiding overleveraging is your balance beam, preventing financial instability. Staying informed and adaptive is your GPS, guiding you through changing financial landscapes. Managing emotions is your steady hand on the tiller, keeping you on course.

Prioritizing long-term goals is your charted destination, leading you through life's financial journey. Balancing risk and reward is your chosen gear, ensuring you're equipped for the financial terrain. Seeking professional advice is your travel guide, offering expertise when needed. Learning from history is your treasure map, revealing the lessons of the past. Building resilience is your sturdy financial bridge, helping you withstand life's unexpected challenges. Understanding economic policies is your compass in the dense financial forest.

Your financial journey is a voyage of discovery, filled with opportunities, challenges, and the promise of financial security. Just as a skilled mariner learns from every wave and every wind, your journey in the world of finance is an ongoing exploration.

With these principles in your arsenal, you're well-prepared to navigate the financial waters. Whether calm or stormy, the financial seas hold potential for growth and success. As you set your course, remember that you are the captain of your financial ship, and with knowledge and wisdom, you can sail with confidence toward your goals.

So, cast off the lines, hoist your financial sails, and set a course for the future. With the lessons learned and the principles embraced, you can chart a path to financial security, success, and prosperity. The journey continues, and the world of finance is waiting to be explored.

Fair winds and following seas on your financial voyage. Set sail with confidence and navigate your financial destiny.

The most important thing is to continue to educate yourself and learn how to invest your money properly.

For this purpose, I highly recommend my other book, "*The Art of Investing*," which is the flagship of my brand.

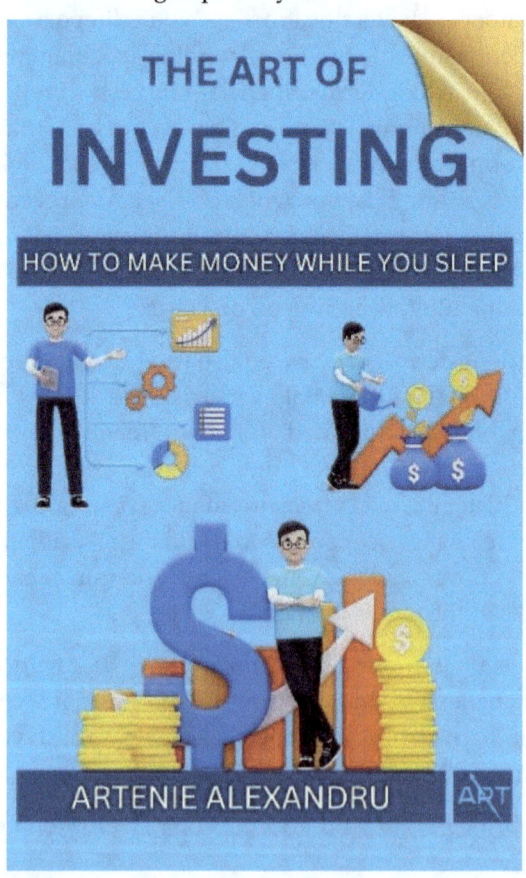

Excerpt from The Art of Investing

Dare to dream about Financial Freedom!

Most people believe financial security means saving as much as possible. In reality, that's not entirely true. Financial security is a combination of saving and investing.

If you just save, there's a good chance you will have to work till your last day. But when you invest, your money grows by itself! And when you add regular investments to your savings, you can take control of your life and plan it.

You did an excellent service to yourself by purchasing this book as a first step.

This is because I will walk you pragmatically through the essential aspects. Then, after reading it, you will be familiar with the most used concepts, be able to do your research, and have your first strategy.

Financial Independence is accessible to you and anybody else!

Check it out on Amazon.

An important investment is Dividends Investing. That is a great approach because it generates passive income, which can finance your life every single month. I encourage you to learn more about it, and so I recommend my book "Live Off Dividends."

Check it on Amazon.

Last but not least, give this book a rating and follow me on Amazon so that others can discover it as well.

I wish you Happy and Successful Investing,

Alexandru Artenie

Claim Your Bonus

Congratulations on reaching out so far!

Get your **7 Checkpoints to Pick a Great Dividend Stock!**

https://www.art-invest.net/dividend-checklist

Join ARTInvest Exclusive Community

You're invited to join our exclusive Facebook group! It's a space for awesome conversations, cool content, and connecting with like-minded folks. We're all about good vibes and interesting chats. Get premium treatment and care, any question is answered and any idea is welcomed!

Click here to join ARTInvest Exclusive Club.

Exclusive Access Code: CrashChronicles

References

1 https://en.wikipedia.org/wiki/Roman_currency

2 https://www.worldhistory.org/Greek_Coinage/

3 https://www.investopedia.com/terms/d/dutch_tulip_bulb_market_bubble.asp

4 https://amsterdamtulipmuseum.com/blogs/tulip-facts/how-were-tulips-traded-so-fast-during-tulip-mania

5 https://amsterdamtulipmuseum.com/pages/semper-augustus-history-s-most-famous-tulip

6 https://amsterdamtulipmuseum.com/blogs/tulip-facts/how-expensive-were-tulips-during-tulip-mania

7 https://en.wikipedia.org/wiki/South_Sea_Company

8 https://fifthperson.com/newtons-south-sea-bubble-chinas-stock-market-crash-history-repeats-itself-294-years-apart/

9 https://www.synergiafoundation.org/insights/analyses-assessments/gold-demand-countries-abandon-us-dollar

10 https://www.semanticscholar.org/paper/The-Real-Estate-and-Stock-Market-During-the-Great-a-Cresap/7a87a483b54e072c3dde1068e00cc2c75793ec5c

11 https://www.economicshelp.org/blog/162985/economics/unemployment-during-the-great-depression/

12 https://www.federalreservehistory.org/essays/oil-shock-of-1973-74

13 https://realeconomy.rsmus.com/that-70s-show-lessons-from-the-oil-shortages-of-50-years-ago/

14 https://en.wikipedia.org/wiki/Volkswagen_Beetle

15 https://oilnow.gy/featured/us-strategic-petroleum-reserves-sink-to-35-year-low/

16 https://labs.sogeti.com/internet-things-bubble-burst-14-years-dotcom-bubble/

17 https://flatworldbusiness.wordpress.com/flat-education/previously/web-1-0-vs-web-2-0-vs-web-3-0-a-bird-eye-on-the-definition/dotcom-bubble/

18 https://www.youtube.com/watch?v=C6ifHxwzk2E

19 https://www.redfin.com/news/next-recession-housing-market/

20 https://www.ccn.com/house-prices-could-tumble-as-much-as-2008-crisis-according-to-new-projection/

21   https://www.cnbc.com/2018/09/10/tell-us-what-you-think-is-the-global-financial-crisis-of-2008-over.html

22 https://www.thebalancemoney.com/2008-financial-crisis-3305679

23https://www.delcampe.net/en_GB/collectables/coins-banknotes/banknotes-euro/100-euro/

24   https://stylemagazine.com/news/2015/feb/13/european-debt-crisis-fast-facts/

25   https://finance.yahoo.com/news/nav-sarao-scapegoat-2010-flash-125022048.html

26   https://www.quantifiedstrategies.com/what-percentage-of-trading-is-algorithmic/

27
https://www.malwarebytes.com/blog/news/2017/11/cryptocurrency-works-cybercriminals-love

28 https://www.pidjin.net/2021/03/19/hodl/

29 https://coinmarketcap.com/

30 https://www.bbc.co.uk/news/business-52050426

31   https://www.cnbc.com/2020/08/20/5-things-to-know-before-the-stock-market-opens-august-20-2020.html

32   https://www.statista.com/chart/21672/financial-responses-to-the-covid-19-pandemic-as-a-share-of-gdp/

33   https://farmdocdaily.illinois.edu/2023/10/the-financial-position-of-the-farm-economy-heading-into-a-higher-interest-rate-macroeconomic-condition.html

www.ingramcontent.com/pod-product-compliance
Lightning Source LLC
Chambersburg PA
CBHW062359290526
45794CB00003B/1006